101 Awful Dad Jokes

———————

Dad Jokes Everywhere!

1. What rock group has
four men that don't sing?
Mount Rushmore.

2. When I was a kid,
my mother told me I could be
anyone I wanted to be.
Turns out, identity theft is a crime.

3. A guy goes to his doctor because he can see into the future. The doctor asks him, "How long have you suffered from that condition?" The guy tells him, "Since next Monday."

4. What concert costs just 45 cents?
50 Cent featuring Nickelback!

5. What do you call a mac 'n' cheese that gets all up in your face?
Too close for comfort food!

6. Why couldn't the bicycle stand up by itself?
It was two tired!

7. Did you hear about the restaurant on the moon?
Great food, no atmosphere!

8. Why do melons have weddings?
Because they cantaloupe!

9. What happens when you go
to the bathroom in France?
European.

10. What's the difference between
a poorly dressed man on a
tricycle and a well-dressed man
on a bicycle?
Attire!

1. How many apples grow on a tree?
All of them!

12. Did you hear the
rumor about butter?
Well, I'm not going to spread it!

13. Did you hear about the guy
who invented Lifesavers?
They say he made a mint!

14. Last night I had a dream
that I weighed less than a
thousandth of a gram.
I was like, Omg.

15. A cheese factory
exploded in France.
Da brie is everywhere!

16. Why did the old man
fall in the well?
Because he couldn't see that well!

17. What do you call a factory that
sells passable products?
A satisfactory!

18. Why did the invisible man
turn down the job offer?
He couldn't see himself doing it!

19. Want to hear a joke
about construction?
I'm still working on it!

20. I was really angry at my friend
Mark for stealing my dictionary.
I told him, "Mark, my words!"

21. How does Moses
make his coffee?
Hebrews it.

22. I'm starting a new
dating service in Prague.
It's called Czech-Mate.

23. I was just reminiscing about the beautiful herb garden I had when I was growing up. Good thymes.

24. Do you know the last thing my grandfather said to me before he kicked the bucket? "Grandson, watch how far I can kick this bucket."

25. I like telling Dad jokes.
Sometimes he laughs!

26. Why did the scarecrow
win an award?
Because he was
outstanding in his field!

27. What do you call a fish
with two knees?
A two-knee fish!

28. Why do you never see
elephants hiding in trees?
Because they're so good at it!

29. Why don't skeletons ever go
trick or treating?
Because they have no body to go
with!

30. This graveyard
looks overcrowded.
People must be dying
to get in there!

31. What's ET short for?
Because he's only got tiny legs!

32. What's brown and sticky?
A stick!

33. Can February march?
No, but April May!

34. What's orange and
sounds like a parrot?
A carrot!

35. How do you make a
Kleenex dance?
Put some boogie in it!

36. Why is Peter Pan always flying?
He Neverlands!

37. What's a ninja's
favorite type of shoes?
Sneakers!

38. What do Santa's elves
listen to ask they work?
Wrap music!

39. Did you hear about the bacon cheeseburger who couldn't stop telling jokes?
It was on a roll.

40. Student: "Can I go to the bathroom?"
Teacher: "It's 'may.'"
Student: "No, it's January."

41. Why was the coach yelling
at a vending machine?
He wanted his quarter back.

42. Why do vampires seem sick?
They're always coffin.

43. Within minutes, the detectives
knew what the murder weapon was.
It was a brief case.

44. To whoever stole my copy of
Microsoft Office, I will find you.
You have my Word!

45. I used to work in a
shoe-recycling shop.
It was sole destroying!

46. My boss told me to have a good
day, so I went home!

47. I'm so good at sleeping I can do
it with my eyes closed!

48. Spring is here!
I got so excited I wet my plants!

49. I thought about going on an all-
almond diet... But that's just nuts!

50. My friend says to me,
"What rhymes with orange?"
And I told him, "No it doesn't!"

51. My wife told me I had to stop acting like a flamingo. So I had to put my foot down!

52. I told my girlfriend she drew her eyebrows too high. She seemed surprised!

53. I tell dad jokes but I have no kids...I'm a faux pa!

54. So a vowel saves another vowel's life. The other vowel says, "Aye E! I owe you!"

55. Did I tell you the time I fell in love during a backflip? I was heels over head!

56. My uncle named his dogs Rolex and Timex. They're his watch dogs!

57. If you see a robbery at an Apple Store does that make you an iWitness?!

58. I would avoid the sushi if I were you. It's a little fishy!

59. Five out of four people admit they're bad with fractions!

60. Two goldfish are in a tank. One says to the other, "Do you know how to drive this thing?"

61. I'll call you later.
Don't call me later, call me Dad!

62. Did you hear about the Italian chef who died?
He pasta way!

63. When the grocery store clerk asks me if I want the milk in a bag, I always tell him, "No, I'd rather drink it out of the carton!"

64. The difference between a numerator and a denominator is a short line. Only a fraction of people will understand this!

65. I don't play soccer
because I enjoy the sport.
I'm just doing it for kicks!

66. I invented a new word today:
Plagiarism!

67. What do you call a
donkey with only three legs?
A wonkey!

68. After dinner, my wife asked if I could clear the table. I needed a running start, but I made it!

69. This morning, Siri said, "Don't call me Shirley."

70. How does a penguin build its house?
Igloos it together!

71. A woman is on trial for beating her husband to death with his guitar collection. The judge asks her, "First offender?" She says, "No, first a Gibson! Then a Fender!"

72. I know a lot of jokes about retired people but none of them work!

73. What do you call a guy
with a rubber toe?
Roberto!

74. What rhymes with
boo and stinks?
You!

75. I accidentally dropped
my pillow on the floor.
I think it has a concushion.

76. Someone complimented my parking today! They left a sweet note on my windshield that said "parking fine."

77. St. Francis worked at Krispy Kreme.
He was a deep friar.

78. In America, using the metric system can get you in legal trouble. In fact, if you sneer at any other method of measuring liquids, you may be held in contempt of quart.

79. I found a wooden shoe in my toilet today.
It was clogged.

80. Some people can't distinguish between etymology and entomology They bug me in ways I can't put into words.

81. My hotel tried to charge me ten dollars extra for air conditioning. That wasn't cool.

82. If an English teacher is
convicted of a crime and
doesn't complete the sentence,
is that a fragment?

83. I think my wife is putting glue
on my antique weapons collection.
She denies it but
I'm sticking to my guns!

84. Which U.S. state is famous for its extra-small soft drinks?
Minnesota!

85. I got a hen to regularly count her own eggs.
She's a real mathamachicken!

86. What did the Ranch say when someone opened the refrigerator door?
"Close the door, I'm dressing!"

87. Why do trees seem
suspicious on sunny days?
They just seem a little shady!

88. What did the policeman
say to his belly button?
You're under a vest!

89. What do you call a fake noodle?
An Impasta!

90. I've been bored recently so I've decided to take up fencing. The neighbors said they will call the police unless I put it back.

91. Why did the math book
look so sad?
Because of all of its problems!

92. I don't really call for funerals that start before noon. I guess I'm just not a mourning person!

93. If two vegans get in a fight, is
it still considered a beef?

94. One of my favorite memories as
a kid was when my brothers used to
put me inside a tire and roll me
down a hill. They were Goodyears!

95. I'M addicted to collecting
vintage Beatles albums.
I need Help!

96. What does the cell say to his
sister when she steps on his toe?
"Oh my toe sis!"

97. I never buy
pre-shredded cheese.
Because doing it yourself is grate.

98. I was playing chess with my
friend and he said,
"Let's make this interesting."
So we stopped playing chess.

99. How do you tell the difference
between a bull and a milk cow?
It is either one or the utter.

100. I have a great joke
about nepotism.
But I'll only tell it to my kids.

101. What do sprinters eat
before a race?
Nothing, they fast!